The Quick and Easy Guide to Mnemonics

Improve Your Memory Instantly with 15 Powerful Memory Aids

Thomas C. Randall

www.ImproveYourMemoryToday.net

Copyright Notice

First Printing, 2012

ISBN-13: 978-1477468869

ISBN-10: 1477468862

Printed in the United States of America

result of putting this information into action in any way, and regardless of your interpretation of the advice.

Foreword

This book is a compact yet comprehensive handbook which includes powerful memory tools that can instantly bring results. These memory aids leverage the underlying principles of how your brain handles and processes information, thus they are bound to work for anyone, regardless of age, gender, level of education or even what you might consider your innate intellectual capability.

My firm conviction is that memory can (and should) be developed, and you will see that your recall seem to dramatically improve after you start using the techniques shared in this book. While that might feel like a miracle to you and seem as though it's the magic power of these techniques which made that possible, it's not. The fact is that you had a great mental capacity all along, and that you were given a glimpse of how incredible your full mental potential could be, if only you will develop it.

While the tools in this book works almost instantly and very well, if you are interested in developing your memory for the long haul and unleashing your full mental potential, you might want to check out my other book, *The Quick and Easy Guide to Memory Improvement: 45 Practical Tips You Can Use to Boost Your Memory*. It covers a lot of ground in the subject of memory improvement, and it shows you practical steps you can take to build your memory both short- and long-term. You can view the book details by visiting www.ImproveYourMemoryToday.net/book.

I will greatly appreciate it if you can let me know what you thought about this book, how helpful it was, any improvements or suggestions to make this book better, or anything. If you liked the book, or if you didn't, let me know via emailing **info@ImproveYourMemoryToday.net** or by leaving a review on the Amazon website. (Go to **www.ImproveYourMemoryToday.net/review2** and you will be taken to the review page directly) You can also get more information on **www.ImproveYourMemoryToday.net**.

Again, thank you for purchasing this guide, and I hope you enjoy your reading!

Thomas C. Randall

Table of Contents

Introduction:
What Is a Mnemonic,
And How Does It Help
Your Memory?

The word mnemonic came from the ancient Greek word μνημονικός (mnēmonikos), meaning "of memory", which is related to the Greek Goddess of memory Mnemosyne. A mnemonic (the first "m" is silent) is, in its simplest terms, any kind of memory aid. In principle, virtually any attempt that you make to remember things better can be referred to as a mnemonic. However, there are some systematic ones that have proven themselves very useful over several decades and even centuries, and you will learn what they are and how to use them in this book. A well-designed mnemonic, like the ones included in this book, will be a great learning technique that helps you memorize things better and improve recall later. You can use mnemonics for anything from facts and figures to names and faces, and you will learn how to do exactly that in this book.

The reason why mnemonics are so powerful is because they leverage each element in the process of forming memory. Namely, they enhance the initial impression and subsequent association, then brings strong visualization in most cases to "cement" the memory. Before we move on, let's briefly touch on each of these elements.

Initial impression. In order to form a strong memory that will be retained for a long time, you need to make sure that the information comes across to your brain as something significant. Visualization is one way of achieving this.

Association. Association is the foundation of every memory. It is how your brain organizes it, stores it, and accesses it later—all by linking the information to something else and making sense of it in relation to the already stored data. You can say that the strength of the association is proportional to the strength of memory. In other words, if something is forgotten easily, that can mean that you failed to form a strong mental connection between it and something else you already know.

Visualization. Humans rely heavily on the visual senses. As you read on, you will understand that the use of multiple senses in an image makes the memory stronger; however, the basis and starting point of using such images for memorizing and recollection is the visual sense.

You will see as you learn the various mnemonics that they all take advantage of these three basic principles.

Okay. Enough of the theory, let's get right into the juicy part.

* To discover more on how your memory works and how you can leverage that information to improve your memory, check out my other book *The Quick and Easy Guide to Memory Improvement:45 Practical Tips You Can Use to Boost Your Memory* (Go to **www.ImproveYourMemoryToday.net/book** for details).

Chapter I.
Linguistic Mnemonics

These techniques involve manipulating words, sentences, and other elements of the language. They are pretty straightforward to learn, intuitive to use and easy to remember. The downside is that it is sometimes hard to come up with something that works for these techniques, which makes the usage narrower compared to other techniques I'll discuss later such as the peg method.

Mnemonic #1. Acronym

a) What is it?

This technique involves forming a new word (aka an acronym) from the first letter or parts of each word of a list.

b) What do you use it for? / How do I use it?

It is used to memorize a list of words.

c) What are some examples?

You can find many such examples in business, among other fields. "SMART" goal setting--that a goal must be Specific, Measurable, Attainable, Relevant, and Time-bound--is a good example.

Or there is the K.I.S.S. principle, which stands for "Keep It Simple, Stupid!"

Mnemonic #2. Acrostic

a) What is it?

In this technique, you form a memorable sentence using the first letters or first few letters from a list of alphabets or words.

b) What do you use it for? / How do I use it?

As noted above, it is used to memorize a list of alphabets or words.

c) What are some examples?

Every Good Boy Does Fine is an acrostic to remember the notes each line of the treble clef represents (E, G, B, D, and F from the bottom up).

I have included other, more clever examples in Chapter V as well.

Mnemonic #3. Rhymes

a) What is it?

This is a technique of using a memorable rhyme which includes the information you want to remember.

b) What do you use it for? / How do I use it?

While it can be used to memorize a list of words, if you are ingenious enough you can use this to memorize almost anything. We will see some brilliant ones in the next chapter.

c) What are some examples?

"Thirty days hath September, April, June, and November" is used to memorize the months which has thirty days in it.

There are some more examples of well-written mnemonic rhymes in Chapter V

Chapter II.
Numerical Mnemonics

These methods use numbers for aiding memory in one way or another. As you will see, you can use these methods to remember something that involves number or even things that doesn't. Even if you consider yourself not good in arithmetic, don't worry. These mnemonics don't have to do much with that. As you'll see, most of the times they are easy to learn and use, yet they are very effective and powerful.

Mnemonic #4. Counts System

a) What is it?

This technique is used to remember a number by forming a phrase in which each word represents each digit of that number. Each word in the phrase contains the same number of characters as in each digit of that number.

b) What do you use it for? / How do I use it?

This is used to remember a number. Although it is more difficult to create a good rhyme and less effective compared to the Major system that will be introduced later in this book, it is easier to use and can be powerful if you have a memorable phrase.

c) What are some examples?

Here is a mnemonic for memorizing the first few digits of Pi:

To 6 decimal places:

"How I wish I could calculate Pi!"

(3 . 1 4 1 5 9 2)

To 7 decimal places:

(suggested in an e-mail from "Professor Amoeba")

"May I have a large container of coffee?"

(3 . 1 4 1 5 9 2 6)

Mnemonic #5. Phone-spell System

a) What is it?

This technique utilizes the number pad on a telephone. You can use to convert words into numbers or vice versa. Incidentally you use this being used all the time in the TV commercials, as companies try to make memorizing their 800 numbers easier. Ever heard of 1-800-flowers? The beauty of this system, when used with phone numbers in particular, is that you don't need to memorize the numbers themselves!

b) What do you use it for? / How do I use it?

As noted above, this can be used to convert words into numbers or numbers into words. However, since one number can represent multiple characters, this will be more effective when used to memorize numbers. Your cellphone can prove to be very handy as a mnemonic generator for this technique, if you are familiar with the auto-complete or word suggestion feature for text messaging. Unfortunately if you own a smartphone that only uses QWERTY keypad, you won't be able to use that.

As easy as this mnemonic is for you to learn and use, there is a big downside to it: that it doesn't use the numbers 1 and 0. That gap would render this technique impractical in many cases.

c) What are some examples?

Let's say you are trying to memorize a ZIP code to which you need send a package. Say the ZIP code is 87246.

If you take a look at the keypad of your phone:

1	2 ABC	3 DEF
4 GHI	5 JKL	6 MNO
7 PQRS	8 TUV	9 WXYZ
*	0	#

You can see that

8: T, U or V

7: P, Q, R or S

2: A, B or C

4: G, H, or I

6: M, N or O.

You can form the word TRAIN with these words. A single word is, arguably, five times easier to memorize than a number with five digits.

Mnemonic #6. Peg Method

a) What is it?

This technique involves a set of visual images you have previously familiarized yourself with, and works by connecting them to individual items in a list. A "peg" is a mental trigger of sorts which will act as a reminder to help you recall the information. Once you memorize and internalize the pegs this method will be very easy and fun to use, and you will learn how to use the images with the examples given below. Moreover, you can use the same system over and over again, which will be a very useful memorization tool that you'll keep for a lifetime.

b) What do you use it for? / How do I use it?

This is primarily used to remember a list. The maximum number of items in the list, as we take a look at the various pegs, varies with the peg you choose to use; generally it is between 10 and around 30 for the systems that I'm about to share. However, as you will see, you can increase the number of items by using a combination of the lists. Also, you will soon learn a powerful method that you can use to create your own peg system which can include hundreds of items.

c) What are some examples?

Let's explore various peg systems, along with actual examples on how to use them.

Mnemonic #6-a. Number-shape Peg

a) What is it?

Before using this peg, like any other peg system, you need to familiarize with a list of words. This particular peg uses numbers from 1 to 10 and an object that resembles the shape of each number. You can use anything that works for you, but here is an example:

The number 1 looks like a *candlestick*
2 - *swan*
3 - *ear*
4 - *sail of a yacht*
5 - *a meat hook*
6 - *a cornet*
7 - *a golf club*
8 - *a snowman*
9 - *a balloon with a string attached*
10(0) - *a hole*

The italicized part is what you need to mentally associate with the corresponding number. Then, you will use these images rather than the numbers themselves in memorizing a list.

b) What do you use it for? / How do I use it?

This peg is most commonly used with a list of less than ten items. Yet, if you are creative enough, you can extend the numbers using the same principle (e.g. the number 11 looks like window panes, etc.) or by using a combination of the images above (an image of an ear being burned by a candlelight for the number 13, etc.). When using the latter, though, you need to be careful because using same symbol multiple times can confuse you.

c) What are some examples?

Here is a sample list of words:

theater, wall, screwdriver, beef, jelly, dentist, poster, store, nurse, leather.

Let's see how you can use the peg system to memorize this list. Basically, you link each word on the list to each peg word, and form a visual image.

1. *theater – candlestick*: A giant **candlestick** in the middle of a **theater**

2. *wall – swan*: A concrete **wall** in the middle of a pond and a **swan** banging its head on the wall

3. *screwdriver – ear*: a **screwdriver** trying to unscrew your **ear**

4. *beef – sail*: A yacht with a red, dripping **sail** made from **beef**

5. *jelly – meat hook*: A giant meat-shaped **jelly** precariously held up by a **meat hook**

6. *dentist – cornet*: A **dentist** trying to perform a dental surgery on a patient with a **cornet**

7. *poster – golf club*: A **poster** being ripped and taken down by a **golf club**

8. *store – snowman*: A **snowman** sliding into a **store**, looking for a coat to warm itself

9. *nurse – balloon*: A **nurse** flying in the sky, holding onto a **balloon**

10. *leather – hole*: A **hole** on a golf course, where the flag is made of **leather**

As we will discuss in the visual mnemonics session, there are certain principles to keep in mind to make the visual images more effective. You might have noticed that the examples above are quite abnormal and outlandish, and there is a reason for that. Your brain responds more readily to novelty than it does to what's mundane. That is, you need to make the image stand out. Here are some ways to achieve that:

Make the image vivid (bright and colorful, exaggerate the elements)

Make it bizarre

Incorporate multiple senses: not only the sight, but the smell, sound, and taste and tactile elements if possible.

Keep these in mind when you use the peg system or any other visual mnemonic technique, and you will increase the effectiveness of the techniques dramatically.

Now, let's look at some other peg systems

Mnemonic #6-b. Number-rhyme Peg

Very similar to the previous one, this peg uses the sound(rhyme) of the numbers rather than the shape(visual image). Here is an example of the rhymes:

The number 1(one) sound like bun
2(two) - shoe
3(three) - tree
4(four) - door
5(five) - hive
6(six) - sticks
7(seven) - heaven
8(eight) - gate
9(nine) -vine
10(ten) - hen

Similar to the last one, this peg can be used to memorize a list of less than ten items. However, this method has one advantage over the last one, because you can come up with another set of rhymes for numbers from 11 to 20, here is an example:

11(eleven) - leaven
12(twelve) - elves (elf)
13(thirteen) - thirsting
14(fourteen) - courting
15(fifteen) - lifting
16(sixteen) - Sistine (Chapel)
17(seventeen) - deafening

18(eighteen) - waiting
19(nineteen) - knighting
20(twenty) - penny

Also, now that you know both the number-shape and number-rhyme pegs, you can combine the two to extend the number of items. For example, you use the number-rhyme method for the first ten items, then use the number-shape method for the next ten items. With just these two techniques, you now have a short-term memory bank of up to 30 items rather than the Magic Number Seven, which is the maximum intrinsic capacity of your conscious brain. For just a couple dozen pages. Now, is that amazing or what?

Mnemonic #6-c. Alphabet-rhyme Peg

This peg includes a list of words that are very similar to the sounds of each alphabet, as you will see below:

A - Hay	J - Jay	S - Espresso
B - Bee	K - Key	T - Tea
C - Sea	L - El	U - Ewe
D - Deer	M - Hem	V - Veal
E - Eve	N - Hen	W - Double You
F - Effort	O - Hoe	X - Ax
G - Jeep	P - Pea	Y - Wire
H - Age	Q - Cue	Z – Zebra
I - Eye	R - Oar	

Use this and the next list for remembering a list with 26 or fewer items.

Mnemonic #6-d. Alphabet-letter Peg

Rather than looking for the closest sound of each alphabet itself, this peg uses words starting with the alphabets. Compared to the last one, this list might be a bit trickier to memorize for the first time, yet less confusing once you have planted them firmly in your brain, because there's no irregularity. Just like any other pegs, this is just an example and you can change some of the words to something that works better for you.

A - Ape	J - Jack	S - Sock
B - Boy	K - Kite	T - Toy
C - Cat	L - Log	U - Umbrella
D - Dog	M - Man	V - Vane
E - Egg	N - Nut	W - Wig
F - Fig	O - Owl	X - X-Ray
G - Goat	P - Pig	Y - Yak
H - Hat	Q - Quill	Z - Zoo
I - Ice	R - Rock	

Mnemonic #7. Major System

a) What is it?

This is a system in which you link a sound and a corresponding alphabet to that sound to numbers. This can be used to create your own pegs for the peg method we've just discussed, or to simply memorize very long numbers such as tens of digits of pi and *e*(root of the natural log). This system is often the "secret" behind extraordinary memory feats demonstrated publicly. Although it might be difficult to learn how to use this system, once you master it, it will be one of the most powerful memory tools in your arsenal.

b) What do you use it for? / How do I use it?

First, you need to learn the phonetic code shown on the next page:

No.	Sounds	Aid for Memory
0	s, z, soft c	z is first letter of zero
1	d, t	The letters have ONE downstroke
2	n	n has TWO downstrokes
3	m	m has THREE downstrokes; also m looks like 3 on its side
4	r	r is is last letter or FOUR.
5	l	L is 50 in Roman numeral
6	sh, j, soft ch, soft g	g is like 6 twisted round
7	k, hard g, q, hard c, hard ch	Imagine K as two 7s rotated and glued together
8	f, ph, v	Script f is like 8
9	b, p	b is like upside-down 9; p is mirror of 9

You need to make sure you know these by heart before you can fully use the technique. Note that the sounds are all consonants; you can add any vowels or *w* and *y* sounds in between the consonants to form a word. When you first learn the system, start with a single- or double- digit numbers and practice converting them into words. The words you use for the single digit numbers from 0 to 9 can be another peg system you can use for the peg method. Here is an example:

0 – saw
1 – toe
2 – knee
3 – ma
4 – ray
5 – law
6 – jaw
7 – cow
8 – fox
9 – bee

Then, as you get better, you can start using this for longer numbers. Most of the time, you will find yourself using 3-to 4-digit combinations for a word.

Although this method is powerful in itself, you can further strengthen your memory by incorporating the visualization methods I'll discuss shortly. I would like to emphasize that this method can be used for anything that involves number, and that the usage of this method is only limited by your creativity. This method can even be a way to convert words into numbers, rather than the other way around, depending on what you're trying to remember.

c) What are some examples?

First, let's see how you can convert two-digit numbers into words:

60 – j + z : jazz

33 – m + m : mom
91 – b + t : bat
08 – s + v : sieve
25 – n + l : nail

You can come up with your own variations, since you can use different letters for each number or different vowels in between.

Let's look at how you can use this method to memorize long numbers. For example, let's use root of natural log *e*:
e = 2.71828182845904...

For the first 15 digits, when you convert the numbers into sounds you get:
e = 2.71828182845904
n k d f n v t f n f r l p s r

Then, you can form these words out of the consonants:
n k d / f n / v t / f n / f r l / p s r
naked / fine / vet / find / frill / passer

Out of these words you can construct a mental image of a **naked**, **fine vet**erinarian running down the street **finds** a piece of cloth with **frills**, while **passer**s-by laugh at this comical scene. This will be a pretty memorable scene, and if you can reconstruct the words in sequence, you will have no problem reverse engineering to the numbers.

Now let's see how you can form your own pegs out of the sound-number pairs. The process is straightforward, because you will simply come up with a word for each number. Building on the list of pegs from 0 to 9, we get:

10 – d + z : doze
11 – d + d : dad
12 – d + n : dune
13 – d + m : dumb
14 – d + r : deer
15 – d + l : duel
16 – d + sh : dish
17 – d + k : duck
18 – d + v : dove
19 – d + p : dip
20 – n + s : nose, etc.

Notice that for the purpose of constructing a peg system, I have used the exact same letter for the first digit. This is important for avoiding confusion, especially when the number of pegs goes beyond a couple dozen. Using the same principle, you can create your own peg system consists of a hundred pegs (0 from 99). That means if your memory of these pegs are strong enough, you can memorize a list of a hundred items without any other aids! If you feel like supercharging this technique, there is a way to take this even further. You can choose one of the pegs introduced earlier (e.g. the number-rhyme peg) and combine that with the 100-peg system that you now have, to form a system of a *thousand* pegs. For example, the number 518 (5+18) can be associated with the image of a dove (18) meddling with a hive (5). For the number 711 (7+11) you can imagine your dad (11) relaxing in the heaven (7) while you hear the angels singing in the background. Just make sure that anything in the 10-peg system (in this case, the number-rhyme peg—bun, shoe, tree...) does not coincide with something in the 100-peg system that you create using the major system.

If you don't want the hassle of creating a hundred pegs from scratch, don't worry. I have included a sample 100-peg system for you in the reference section.

Mnemonic #8. Dominic System

a) What is it?

Named after its inventor and several-time memory world champion Dominic O'Brien, This is a system used to remember sequences of numbers. The purpose and methodology is similar to the Major system, in that it uses assigned alphabets or "initials" for each digit; however, this method uses people(celebrities) and actions, rather than objects, as representations of a pair of digits. A very interesting element of this method is that a pair of digits not only represents a celebrity but an action commonly associated with that individual, out of which you can make a story. You will see what this means in a minute, as I explain how to use this method below.

b) What do you use it for? / How do I use it?

As mentioned earlier, this method is used to remember a list of numbers. Before using the method, you need to learn the number-"initial" code:

No.	Initial	Aid for Memory
1	A	First five letters of the alphabet
2	B	
3	C	
4	D	
5	E	
6	S	S for Six*
7	G	G is the seventh letter of the alphabet.
8	H	H is the eighth letter of the alphabet; also, H sounds similar to "eight"
9	N	N for Nine
0	O	They look similar; also, 0 is sometimes read as "o"

* Note: from numbers 1 to 8 except 6, they all correspond to the first 8 letters of the alphabet in order. So memorize "A-B-C-D-E-**S**-G-H", as S sounds somewhat similar to F.

Now let's look at how you convert numbers into people and actions

(number – initial – person – action)
23 – BC – Bill Cosby – Stand-up comedy
16 – AS – Arnold Schwarzenegger –
Terminator firing rifles
43 – DC – David Copperfield – Performing magic
91 – NA – Neil Armstrong – Landing on Moon

The person you choose does not have to be a celebrity; it can be a character in a movie, someone you know, a historic figure, or any entity that has some kind of relationship with the initials. For example, 63(SC) can be Santa Claus!

Remember, as this is designed to help you, not distract you or make things difficult. So, if you can't think of anyone who has that initial, just make up something! If you're stuck with the initial OD, just imagine an Old Dog! Modify the system all you like to make it serve you.

c) What are some examples?

Let's say you are trying to remember the number 2316. You can imagine Bill Cosby firing rifles on a stage. For longer numbers, you can create a story out of the people and actions. For example, if the number you're trying to remember is 23164391, you can imagine that Bill Cosby firing a gun on a stage, then David Copperfield, who was in the audience, escaping the scene by landing on Moon.

As you have seen, while the pairs can either be represented by a person or an action, most of the times it will be the easiest when you place them in an alternating order. Like many other methods, you can combine this method with other mnemonics to further strengthen the recall. For example, the Method of Loci or the journey method, which I'll introduce shortly, can be a good accompaniment to this method.

Chapter III.
Visual Mnemonics

Although the peg method covered earlier is an effective mnemonic, the reason why it works so well does not have to do with the strength of the pegs themselves. Sure, it would be much easier for you to memorize number-rhyme pegs than pegs created from the major system, but once you internalize them, the latter works just as well as the former. In the peg method, pegs are just tools to take you to the important part—visualization. Regardless of the particular system you use, virtually every time you use the peg method you will rely on creating visual image, and that's where your brain really responds to the input.

In this section you will be introduced to what I call visual mnemonics, and as the name suggests, these mnemonics all have visualization at their core. These are sound and effective methods in themselves, and will be even more powerful if used in conjunction with one or more of the other mnemonics discussed so far.

Mnemonic #9. Method of Loci

a) What is it?

Also known as the Roman Room method, this was used by the Romans to remember information, most of the times long speeches. The great Greek and Roman orators first created mnemonics and used them a lot because usually there were no other memory aids that came in handy. This seeming disadvantage led them to invest in making good mental devices (i.e. mnemonics) that will allow them to memorize hours' worth of material without notes or other cues. This is one of such products, where you memorize information by mentally placing things you want to remember in a room that you are familiar with.

b) What do you use it for? / How do I use it?

This is an effective method of remembering information without particular structure, and you can use this for almost any form of information.

Using this technique is simple and does not require much time until you can use it. As mentioned earlier, you need to have a mental picture of a room (or any other physical location that you are familiar with). Then, mentally place the objects that symbolize the information you are trying to remember alongside the things that have already been in the room.

There are several tips you want to keep in mind to increase the effectiveness of this technique. First, you need to take time producing a clear image of the location you are going to use. Then, take note of particular objects which will be used as triggers, such as the desk and bookshelf in your study, or the couch and coffee table in your living room. The more the number of these objects, the more "memory slots" you have. Finally, try to place the objects in a way that makes as much sense to you as possible.

Here are couple more considerations for you in using the Method of Loci. The reference does not have to be a room per se. If you feel like using something else such as a landscape is more effective for you, you can populate that with the symbolic objects. Also, you can expand this technique to multiple rooms in a house, for structuring and storing information in several categories. If you do this, make sure the atmosphere and arrangement of each room appropriately represent the overall theme of its respective category, and the differentiation between one room to another is meaningful enough to prevent confusion and mixing up in your memory.

c) What are some examples?

Let's use the following hypothetical shopping list to show you how you can use the Method of Loci:

broccoli, carrots, salad, bread, cereal, kitchen paper, salmon, chicken thighs, pork chops, canned soup, cantaloupe, bath tub cleaner.

Now, say you are using your living room as the place for the method, which has the following objects:

coffee table, lamp, couch, TV, CD rack, DVD player, large bookcase, small bookcase, telephone, rocking chair, picture on the wall

You can simply place the items from your shopping list on these objects. For example:

broccoli – coffee table: a large broccoli stalk growing from the coffee table
carrots – lamp: a carrot dangling off of the lamp
salad – couch: leafy veggies all over your couch
bread – TV: a TV commercial featuring the type of the bread you want to buy
cereal – CD rack: a box of your favorite cereal brand conspicuously protruding from the rack

I think you get the point. Like any other mnemonic that involves visualization, it can be quite fun coming up with a bizarre image for the items. Use this method often, and you will notice yourself getting better and better. You might even find yourself enjoying having something to remember because you can use these fun methods!

Mnemonic #10. Journey Method

a) What is it?

This method is very similar to the Method of Loci in that it involves mentally placing objects in certain physical locations. The difference between the two is that while you "stand still" in your imagination for the Method of Loci, in this method you go on a journey along a route that you are familiar with, as its name indicates.

b) What do you use it for? / How do I use it?

While this method is very similar to the Method of Loci, the purposes of using them can be different. Since taking a journey involves an element of timing and sequence, you can leverage this method for remembering a sequential list. Or, you can strategically arrange the order of the list in advance so that the most important items come first in the journey

Another big advantage of this method is that it can be used to remember quite long lists. The "journey" here can either be a short trip or long journey true to its name, yet once you are familiar enough with the landmarks and details of the journey the length of it wouldn't be a limitation at all. Also, you can extend or shorten the journey depending on the length of the list, which makes it very flexible.

Like the Method of Loci, it is highly recommended that you take time to mentally follow and/or construct the journey in advance, and designate what elements of it will function as landmarks, or "hooks" to which you will connect the items you want to remember. To start out, choose something that is familiar to you, such as your commute to work every morning, or the route to visit your grandparents. Go through the journey in your imagination, and try identifying objects that can act as landmarks. You can even put things that aren't there in reality—as long as it makes sense and works for you, it can only help you.

If it helps to write down the list of landmarks and the order in which they appear, by all means do so. Consider this as an investment which will pay dividends for your lifetime. In fact, the clearer you can imagine the journey in your mind, the more effective the method will be. Writing down and checking twice helps you get that clarity.

After you have designated the landmarks, go through the journey one more time, this time paying attention and noting the landmarks and checking the order in which they appear. Do this several times until you can recall the journey and notice all the landmarks in the right order. Then, you can freely wield the power of this method for remembering any information you'd like.

c) What are some examples?

Using the same shopping list from the previous example, let's see how you can use the journey method. Here's the list again:

broccoli, carrots, salad, bread, cereal, kitchen paper, salmon, chicken thighs, pork chops, canned soup, cantaloupe, bath tub cleaner.

Since this particular list is a shopping list, let's use the route you take from your home to the supermarket. For example:

Garage door: a **broccoli** stalk is dangling upside down on the door

Your car: you notice that instead of the wipers, there are two sticks of **carrot** on your windshield

Driveway: there are **leafy veggies** everywhere! Even worse, there's dressing on them!

On the sidewalk: the curbs are made of sliced **breads**

Get the idea? Have fun with the method and use it often, and you will be well on your way to perfecting the art of memorizing with this method!

Mnemonic #11. Linking

a) What is it?

Linking, another visualization method, is a technique of directly connecting one item in the list to the next without external hooks such as objects in a room or landmarks along a route. This method is very intuitive and easy to use. Essentially you'll make a story out of the items; yet the story does not have to be logical—it just needs to flow smoothly from one item to another. As a matter of fact, the more illogical and outlandish the "story" is, the more memorable it will be for you!

b) What do you use it for? / How do I use it?

This is primarily used for remembering a list of words or names, with or without a sequence. The biggest upside of this technique is that you don't need to learn or prepare anything in advance. However, you need to make sure that the images you make out of the words are as vivid and memorable as possible, because the images are the only cue for recall this method depends upon. Having said that, you can substitute certain words in the list to another word which reminds you of the original, if the substitute word creates a better image for you.

How to use method is best described with an example, so let's go ahead and look at one.

c) What are some examples?

This example is taken from my other book, *The Quick and Easy Guide to Memory Improvement: 45 Practical Tips You Can Use to Boost Your Memory.* You will get more comprehensive advice on how to give a quick boost for your memory short-term and build it up on a solid ground long-term. You can get the book by visiting **www.ImproveYourMemoryToday.net/book.**

Let's say the first four words of a list you are trying to remember are *window, flounder, marble and volcano.*

Start with yourself sitting in your living room looking out the **window**. Then, out of the blue, a giant **flounder** flies in through the window, shattering it with a clanging noise. After twisting in pain, the flounder gags and spits out several pieces of shining **marbles**. You pick up one of the marbles, and when you look into it you see a **volcano** erupting, and you can almost feel the heat and the shaking of the ground...

Chapter IV.
Putting 'em All Together

The following methods were developed by Mark D'Arcy, author of *Introducing Mnemonics*. They integrate multiple methods that you have learned so far and are very useful for the specific purpose that they were intended to serve. Using these methods can be a fun experience for you, as well as educational. You will find how you can use the mnemonics you've learned so far to other purposes, such as learning a foreign language and remembering names and faces.

Mnemonic #12. Remembering Mathematical Formulae

a) What is it?

It is a system for remembering mathematical formula. It uses the alphabet-rhyme peg (and/or the alphabet-letter peg, whichever one suits you better) and visualization methods.

b) What do you use it for? / How do I use it?

First you need to learn some more pegs for the mathematical symbols:

+ : window frame
- : canal
x : kiss
/ : tennis court
√ : chair
= : double-decker bus

Then, you use the alphabet-rhyme peg and these pegs together to form a mental image to represent a formula. In some cases, you might need to come up with additional pegs to represent Greek alphabets and other method of computations, such as log. (Incidentally, you can simply imagine a log in this case!)

An additional tip is that, because in many cases in scientific formula the case matters, so you might want to use both types of the alphabet peg for the purpose of distinguishing uppercase and lowercase. This is not mandatory if you can correctly remember the cases, but this one tip can prove to be very useful when you are faced with a complex formula with lots of variables in it.

c) What are some examples?

Let's see how you can apply this system to a formula. Take the famous $E=mc^2$. And let's use the alphabet-rhyme peg for the lowercase letters and the alphabet-letter peg for the uppercase, which gives the following:

E: egg
=: double-decker bus
m: hem
c: sea

there are many ways to handle the "squared" part. You can choose to use a peg for the number 2 among the number pegs introduced earlier, yet I think that can cause some confusion because you don't know whether the number means "times two" or "squared". In this case, I will use an image of a square sea, or "sea squared".

Okay, so let's come up with an image for this formula. A double-decker bus filled with eggs, driving along the hem of a giant pair of jeans, which leads to a square-shaped sea!

Since the formula was too short it might have seemed that you can memorize this formula without this system; however, I guarantee you this will be of great help for you if you use it for more complex ones. Just try it and see the difference for yourself.

Mnemonic #13. Mental Diary

a) What is it?

This is a system for remembering appointments and schedules, as the name of it suggests. Using the peg systems introduced earlier along with the new one that will be discussed in a moment, you will be able to remember important events without additional aids.

b) What do you use it for? / How do I use it?

First, you want to learn a new set of pegs representing the days of the week:

Monday – moon
Tuesday – tube
Wednesday – (magic) wand
Thursday – thorn
Friday – (French) fries
Saturday – satellite dish
Sunday – sundae

You can call this "day/rhyme peg", and again you can come up with your own if that serves you better. Now you need to choose two peg systems for remembering the hour and the minute.

For the hour, there are two choices; you can choose to use the 24-hour system or 12-hour system. Obviously, you would need a 24-peg system for the former and a 12-peg system for the latter along with an additional mental hook for denoting AM and PM(often times just picturing the scene as taking place in the day or at night will do). I personally think 12-hour system is better because it involves lesser number of pegs. However, if you have a peg system that you've internalized well, and you are more used to using 24-hour system in your daily life, you might find it work better for you.

For the minute, I advise you to take a look at the 100-peg system (made from the Major System) included in the reference section, and use the first 60 pegs. (The pegs work very well and you can use them for various purposes, so I strongly suggest you commit the system to memory. Revisiting the section on Major System will help your memorizing.)

Finally, you need to designate an image which symbolizes the event or appointment itself. Just picturing yourself doing the activity will suffice. Then, you have one peg each for the day, the hour, the minute, and the activity, you can construct an entry in your mental diary.

c) What are some examples?

Let's say you are playing racquetball with your friends on Saturday at 10:15am. Supposing you are using number/rhyme peg and the 100-peg system from the following chapter for hour and minute, respectively, you have:

Day: Saturday – satellite dish

Hour: 10am – hen

Minute: 15 – duel

Now, you can come up with a funny image that goes like this:

On a giant **satellite dish**, you see two **hens** in a **duel**, but the funny thing is that instead of using a pistol, they are hitting each other with a **racquetball racquet**!

Mnemonic #14. Learning a Foreign Language

a) What is it?

This is a mnemonic system for memorizing vocabulary from a foreign language.

b) What do you use it for? / How do I use it?

You convert the whole or parts of a word from a foreign language to an English word or words similar in pronunciation. Then you use one of the visual mnemonics introduced earlier to form an image, including the original meaning of the foreign word.

c) What are some examples?

In Spanish, the word **cabina** means phone booth. You can simply turn this into an image by playing with the words:

cabina = phone booth becomes *cab-in-a-phone-booth*!

The next time you hear the word **cabina**, you will be instantly triggered to picture a cab trying to fit into a **phone booth**, then you will have no problem remembering the meaning of the word!

Mnemonic #15. Remembering Names and Faces

a) What is it?

This is a technique of using the mnemonics for remembering people's names.

b) What do you use it for? / How do I use it?

Before I go into explaining how you can use mnemonics for remembering names, I'd like to briefly share with you some basic tips that will help you remember names better:

- Pay attention to the facial features of the person. See if anything stands out, be it forehead, eyebrows, nose, mouth, jaw, etc.
- Ask the person if they could repeat the name when you are introduced to him/her.
- Use his/her name in conversation to help strengthen the connection.

On top of these tips, you can try using their names as a subject for a mnemonic. One way is to visualize someone you already know with the same first name (if there is one) with the person you just met. Mentally observe as you introduce them and their being pleasantly surprised to find someone with a same name. Another is to find a word that rhymes with or reminds you of either their first or last name, and form a mental image which includes them and the word together. You can form a more effective picture if you can relate the word it to their unique facial features you have taken a note of. I'll give you an example of how to do that.

c) What are some examples?

Suppose you meet a new person, and her name is Shirley Jackson. Let's say she happened to have a curly hair, and you can make a rhyme mnemonic that goes like: "Shirley with a curly hair".

Or, you can imagine her dressed and dancing like the famous pop singer Michael Jackson, making the image a cue for remembering her last name. For this technique, you can use the last name of practically any celebrity or historical figure you know.

Chapter V.
More Examples

Here are some clever mnemonics to remember various facts, along with a compilation of various pegs and other details presented so far. You can use these as an inspiration to come up with your own nifty mnemonic, or you can simply choose to enjoy while your friends watch you in awe as you perform a seemingly amazing feat of memory!

Example #1. Memorizing Roman Numerals (Rhyme)

Here's a mnemonic rhyme written by Peter Hobbs that booth explains and helps you memorize the 7 basic roman numerals (I, V, X, L, C, D and M):

M's "mille", or **1000** said
D's half, **500** - quickly read!
C's just a century! (**100**)
and **L**'s half again – **50**!
So all that's left is **X** and **V**,
or **10** and **5** - and I - easy!

Example #2. U.S. Land Acquisitions Since 1803 (Acrostic)

Lora M. Gomez wrote a useful mnemonic for recalling the locations of every territorial acquisition by the United States of America from 1803 onwards:

"**L**ittle **P**eople, **WE T**alk **O**f **M**ister **G**reen
At **H**ome
Pouring **G**reen **W**ater **A**round **C**old **V**ases "

indicating:
Louisiana **P**urchase (1803)
West Florida (annexed 1812)
East Florida (annexed 1819)
Texas (annexed 1845)
Oregon Country (1846)
Mexican Cession (1848)
Gadsden Purchase (1853)
Alaska (purchased 1867)
Hawaii (annexed 1898)
Puerto Rico (ceded 1898)
Guam (ceded 1898)
Wake Island (annexed 1899)
American Samoa (annexed 1899)
Canal Zone (leased 1903)
Virgin Islands (1917)

Example #3. Books of the Old Testament (Rhyme)

Here's a mnemonic rhyme of unknown origin that includes all 39 books of the Old Testament in order:

The great Jehovah speaks to us
In Genesis and Exodus;
Leviticus and Numbers see,
Followed by Deuteronomy.

Joshuah and Judges sweep the land,
Ruth gleans a sheaf with trembling hand;
Samuel and numerous Kings appear,
Whose Chronicles we wondering hear.

Ezra and Nehemiah now,
Esther the beauteous mourner show,
Job speak in sighs, David in Psalms,
The Proverbs teach to scatter alms.

Ecclesiastes then comes on,
And the sweet Song of Solomon.
Isiah, Jeremiah then
With Lamentations takes his pen.

Ezekiel, Daniel, Hosea's lyres,
Swell Joel, Amos, Obadiah's.
Next Jonah, Micah, Nahum come,
And lofty Habbakuk finds room.

While Zephaniah, Haggai calls,

Rapt Zechariah builds his walls,
And Malachi, with garments rent,
Concludes the ancient testament.

Example #4. Spelling Rules (Rhyme)

Here is a standard mnemonic rhyme for spelling English words which will sort out a lot of confusion:

i before e - except after c
or when sounding like a as in neighbor and weigh

For example, the words 'pieces' and 'caddie' use ie, while 'ceiling', 'receive' and 'freight' use the reverse.

A new mnemonic by Peter Hobbs illustrates how "seize" is a rare exception to the rule, where unlike in the standard "siege", one applies the unexpected!

*Note: there are a few exceptions to this rule. However, a brilliant sentence written by Barbara D. Martin includes nearly all of them:

"Neither ancient foreign sheikh seized the weird heights."

Example #5. The Zodiac Signs (Rhyme)

English hymn-writer Isaac Watts (1674-1748) wrote the following verse for remembering the 12 zodiac signs in order:

The RAM, the BULL, the heavenly TWINS,
And next the CRAB, the LION shines,
The VIRGO and the SCALES; The SCORPION,
ARCHER and SEA-GOAT,
The MAN who pours the water out
And FISH with glittering tails.

* The date and symbol for 12 zodiac sign are:

Sign	Symbol	Date
Aries	ram	Mar 21~Apr 20
Taurus	bull	Apr 21~May 20
Gemini	twins	May 21~Jun 20
Cancer	crab	Jun 21~Jul 22
Leo	lion	Jul 23~Aug 22
Virgo	virgin	Aug 23~Sep 22
Libra	scales	Sep 23~Oct 22
Scorpio	scorpion	Oct 23~Nov 22
Sagittarius	archer	Nov 23~Dec 22
Capricorn	sea-goat	Dec 23~Jan 20
Aquarius	water-bearer	Jan 21~Feb 19

In closing...

I hope you have enjoyed reading this book, and are already busy practicing the mnemonics and experiencing the benefits. These are powerful tools that can bring you long-lasting benefits once you put in the initial work mastering them.

If you have enjoyed this book, I will greatly appreciate if you can leave me an honest review (to leave a review on Amazon, visit the following link: **www.ImproveYourMemoryToday.net/review2**) or tell your friends about this book. That way, I can make sure that you are doing great with the information shared in this book, and that others can benefit from this book too.

In fact, I'll send you a PDF version of the reference portion that follows to you if you leave an honest review on Amazon and send a screenshot to **review@ImproveYourMemoryToday.net**. Please title your e-mail message "RE: review screenshot", in order to make sure it gets through the anti-spam filter. The PDF form will come in very handy for you.

Or if you just have any questions or would like more information on other tips on memory improvement or future book releases, you can write to **info@ImproveYourMemoryToday.net** or visit **www.ImproveYourMemoryToday.net**. I'll be looking forward to hearing from you!

Also, if you want a more comprehensive guide on how to build your memory on a strong foundation, check out my other book *The Quick and Easy Guide to Memory Improvement:45 Practical Tips You Can Use to Boost Your Memory*

(Go to **ImproveYourMemoryToday.net/book** to find out more about the book). It is full of practical advice and tips, and you'll be shown how to implement those in real life with the accompanying exercises.

In the meantime, take care, and good luck with whatever you will do with your improved memory!

Thomas C. Randall

Reference

Keypad for Phone-spell system

1	2 ABC	3 DEF
4 GHI	5 JKL	6 MNO
7 PQRS	8 TUV	9 WXYZ
*	0	#

Sample 100-peg system from the major system

0 – saw 1 – toe 2 – knee 3 – ma 4 – ray
5 – law 6 – jaw 7 – cow 8 – fox 9 – bee

10 – doze 11 – dad 12 – dune 13 – dumb 14 – deer
15 – duel 16 – dish 17 – duck 18 – dove 19 – dip

20 – noose 21 – net 22 – nun 23 – gnome 24 – Nero
(Roman Emperor)
25 – nail 26 – notch 27 – neck 28 – knife 29 – knob

30 – mice 31 – mud 32 – moon 33 – mom 34 – mower
35 – mail 36 – mash 37 – mic 38 – movie 39 – map

40 – rose 41 – rat 42 – rain 43 – ram 44 – rear
45 – rail 46 – rush 47 – wreck 48 – roof 49 – rope

50 – lass 51 – loot 52 – lane 53 – lime 54 – lure
55 – lily 56 – leech 57 – leek 58 – lava 59 – lip

60 – chess 61 – chat 62 – chin 63 – chime 64 - chair
65 – chill 66 – cha cha 67 – chalk 68 – chief 69 – chip

70 – case 71 – cat 72 – can 73 – comb 74 – car
75 – cool 76 – cash 77 – coke 78 – cave 79 – cub

80 – fuzz 81 – foot 82 – fan 83 – foam 84 – fire
85 – fall 86 – fish 87 – fog 88 – fife 89 – fob

90 – bus 91 – bat 92 – bone 93 – beam 94 – beer
95 – ball 96 – bush 97 – book 98 – beef 99 – bib

Summary of numerical pegs

No	N-S	N-R	N-R2	M	D
1	candle-stick	bun	leaven	d, t	A
2	swan	shoe	elves	n	B
3	ear	tree	thirsting	m	C
4	sail (yacht)	door	courting	r	D
5	meat hook	hive	lifting	l	E
6	cornet	sticks	Sistine (Chapel)	sh, j, soft ch, soft g	S
7	golf club	Heaven	deafening	k, hard g, q, hard c, hard ch	G
8	snow-man	gate	waiting	f, ph, v	H
9	balloon	vine	knighting	b, p	N
10 (0)	hole	hen	penny	s, z, soft c	O

* Note
N-S: Number-shape
N-R: Number-rhyme
N-R2: Number-rhyme, 11-20
M: Major system
D: Dominic system

Alphabetic pegs

	A-R	A-L		A-R	A-L
A	Hay	Ape	**N**	Hen	Nut
B	Bee	Boy	**O**	Hoe	Owl
C	Sea	Cat	**P**	Pea	Pig
D	Deer	Dog	**Q**	Cue	Quill
E	Eve	Egg	**R**	Oar	Rock
F	Effort	Fig	**S**	Espresso	Sock
G	Jeep	Goat	**T**	Tea	Toy
H	Age	Hat	**U**	Ewe	Umbrella
I	Eye	Ice	**V**	Veal	Vane
J	Jay	Jack	**W**	Double You	Wig
K	Key	Kite	**X**	Ax	X-Ray
L	El	Log	**Y**	Wire	Yak
M	Hem	Man	**Z**	Zebra	Zoo

* A-R: Alphabet-rhyme, A-L: Alphabet-letter

Other pegs

Mathematical symbols

+	window frame	-	canal	x	kiss
/	tennis court	√	chair	=	double-decker bus

Peg for Mental Diary

Day	Peg
Monday	moon
Tuesday	tube
Wednesday	(magic) wand
Thursday	thorn
Friday	(French) fries
Saturday	satellite dish
Sunday	sundae

For more information, visit

www.ImproveYourMemoryToday.net
email: **info@ImproveYourMemoryToday.net**

Leave a review on Amazon:
www.ImproveYourMemoryToday.net/review2

Also from the author:
The Quick and Easy Guide to Memory Improvement: 45 Practical Tips You Can Use to Boost Your Memory
(Go to
www.ImproveYourMemoryToday.net/book to find out more**)**

Made in the USA
Charleston, SC
10 June 2012